Business Administration Scale

Family Child Care

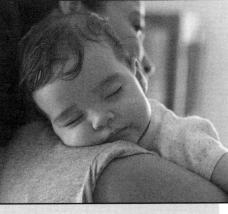

Second Edition

TEACHERS COLLEGE PRESS

TEACHERS COLLEGE | COLUMBIA UNIVERSITY

NEW YORK AND LONDON

Teri N. Talan, J.D., Ed.D, and

Paula Jorde Bloom, Ph.D.

Published by Teachers College Press, 1234 Amsterdam Avenue, New York, NY 10027

Cover photos by (L to R): Weekend Images Inc. / gpointstudio / monkeybusinessimages, all via iStock by Getty Images.

ISBN 978-0-8077-5939-4 (paperback)

Printed on acid-free paper
Manufactured in the United States of America

25   24   23   22   21   20   19   18   8   7   6   5   4   3   2   1

Training is available from the McCormick Center for Early Childhood Leadership (McCormickCenter@nl.edu) for practitioners, mentors, researchers, and program evaluators to help ensure the most reliable use of the *Business Administration Scale for Family Child Care*. Contact Dr. Teri Talan, McCormick Center for Early Childhood Leadership, National Louis University, 6200 Capitol Drive, Wheeling, Illinois, 60090, 800/443-5522, ext. 5060 or teri.talan@nl.edu.

Contents

Acknowledgments

Since the publication of the first edition of the *Business Administration Scale for Family Child Care* (BAS) in 2009, we have had the honor of working with hundreds of family child care providers, technical assistance specialists, quality assessors, and policymakers from across the United States. These individuals participated in professional learning opportunities ranging from conference sessions to intensive, four-day BAS reliability training. Many of these individuals continued the reliability journey and became certified BAS assessors so that they could collect data for research, quality monitoring, technical assistance, or coaching. It was their clarifying questions, using the BAS in the field with family child care providers, that inspired most of the revisions found in this second edition. We want to acknowledge the importance of this feedback from practitioners and express our thanks to all the training participants who made a contribution to the second edition of the *Business Administration Scale for Family Child Care*.

The impetus for the development of the *Business Administration Scale for Family Child Care* (BAS) came from our experience using the *Program Administration Scale* (PAS), first published in 2004. The PAS was designed to measure, monitor, and improve the quality of leadership and management practices in center-based early care and education programs. Whenever we provided intensive training on how to use the PAS to improve program quality, we were asked by participants, "What about a tool to improve the quality of business practices in family child care?" This repeated request convinced us of the need for a valid and reliable instrument to measure the quality of business and professional practices in family child care settings.

In July 2007, Illinois officially launched a quality rating system, Quality Counts–QRS, which included the BAS as one of two measures of program quality in family child care. The Illinois Department of Human Services (IDHS) provided us with time and resources to pilot the BAS and gather data for our reliability and validity study of the instrument. We are indebted to IDHS for their continuing support of our work and their commitment to improving the quality of business and professional practices in family child care settings in Illinois.

Data collection in Illinois continued throughout 2008. Data were also gathered in Tennessee, Florida, and California with the assistance of the Tennessee Early Childhood Training Alliance (TECTA), the Miami-Dade United Way Center for Excellence, and the Riverside County Child Care Coalition. We appreciate their collective contributions to the development of this instrument. We want to express our gratitude to the W. Clement and Jesse V. Stone Foundation for providing support to generate the 2009 national norms for the BAS and for their belief in the value of our work.

Several family child care experts helped us in the development of the *Business Administration Scale for Family Child Care* by reviewing drafts of the manuscript. Our heartfelt thanks go to Michelle Bossers, Ida Butler, Tom Copeland, Linda Hermes, Kathy Modigliani, Joe Perrault, and Barbara Sawyer for their helpful insights. A special thank you as well to the family child care providers who participated in our focus groups and graciously gave their time, shared their documents, and welcomed our research team into their homes.

We are so appreciative of the commitment and hard work of the research team involved in the reliability and validity studies of the BAS—Linda Butkovich, Shirley Flath, Ann Hentschel, Renita Johnson, Lilian Perez, and Kathleen Radice. We are deeply indebted to Michael Abel, Robyn Kelton, Diana Schaack, and Jion Yen for their statistical support. Their expertise was indispensable in conducting the psychometric analyses of the BAS.

Special thanks to the BAS national anchors—Jill Bella, Linda Butkovich, Melissa Casteel, and Robyn Kelton—for their expertise in responding to questions from the field, critical consideration of needed revisions, and review of the final manuscript, and to Kelley May for her assistance in preparing the document for publication. Finally, we want to recognize Sarah J. Biondello, our editor at Teachers College Press, for her support, patience, and appreciation of the intricacies involved in revising this assessment tool.

Overview of the Business Administration Scale

Rationale

The genesis of the *Business Administration Scale for Family Child Care* (BAS) was the growing professional consensus that the quality of family child care is determined by more than a provider's nurturing heart and caring interactions with children. While there were several instruments available to measure the quality of provider-child interactions and the quality of the learning environment, there wasn't a valid and reliable instrument that measured the business practices in family child care settings. The *Business Administration Scale for Family Child Care* was designed to fill that void.

Research on family child care indicates that providers who utilize effective professional and business practices are less likely to experience personal and professional stress and more likely to view family child care as a career. They are also more likely to provide a high-quality learning environment and interact more sensitively with children (Abell, Arsiwalla, Putnam, & Miller, 2014; Bordin, Machida, & Varnell, 2000; Forry, et al., 2013; Hallam, Bargreen, & Ridgley, 2013; Helburn, Morris, & Modigliani, 2002; Hughes-Belding, Hegland, Stein, Sideris, & Bryant, 2012; Kontos, Howes, Shinn, & Galinsky, 1996; Raikes, et al., 2013).

The *Business Administration Scale for Family Child Care* was designed to serve as a reliable and easy-to-administer tool for measuring and improving the overall quality of business and professional practices in family child care settings. The development of the BAS began with a review of the literature on best practices in family child care with an eye to policies and practices that support the well-being and professionalism of providers, as well as positive outcomes for children and families.

The content of the BAS reflects the wisdom in the field about the components of high-quality family child care. High-quality programs are run by providers who are intentional in their work with children and families, committed to ongoing professional development, engaged in ethical practice, and savvy about accessing community resources to support families and to enhance the effectiveness of their programs. High-quality programs have business practices and policies in place that promote financial stability, reduce the risk associated with doing business in a home environment, and comply with local and state legal requirements (NAFCC, 2013).

The BAS includes 37 indicator strands clustered in 10 items. The instrument was constructed to complement the widely used *Family Child Care Environment Rating Scale–Revised* (FCCERS-R) by Harms, Cryer, and Clifford (2007). Both the BAS and the FCCERS-R measure quality on a 7-point scale, and both generate a profile to guide program improvement efforts. When used together, these instruments provide a comprehensive picture of the quality of the family child care learning environment and the business practices that undergird the program.

Multi-Use Design

The *Business Administration Scale for Family Child Care* is applicable for multiple uses: program self-improvement, technical assistance and monitoring, professional development, research and evaluation, and public awareness. The target audience for the BAS is family child care providers and those working to monitor and improve the quality of family child care business and professional practices.

- ◆ **Self-improvement**. Because indicators are objective and quantifiable on a 7-point continuum from inadequate to excellent, providers can easily set goals to incrementally improve business practices. The resulting profile can be used to benchmark a provider's progress in meeting goals over time.

- **Technical assistance and monitoring**. As part of local or state quality enhancement initiatives, the BAS can serve as a convenient technical assistance tool providing clear guidelines for incrementally improving professional and business practices to ensure high-quality family child care.

- **Professional development.** The BAS provides a broad overview of professional and business best practices in family child care settings, reinforcing the important role that providers play in determining the quality of care and education. The BAS is used as a text in early childhood courses.

- **Research and evaluation.** For independent research studies or publicly funded quality rating systems that reward higher levels of quality, the BAS can be used to describe current levels of quality in the area of business and professional practice, as well as benchmark changes over time.

- **Public awareness.** Because the BAS is written in clear language and provides a rubric of concrete examples, it can help inform stakeholders—providers, training specialists, agency administrators, policymakers, resource and referral specialists, and parents—about the professional and business components of high-quality family child care.

Items, Indicator Strands, and Indicators

The BAS measures quality on a 7-point scale in 10 items. The first 9 items relate to all family child care programs. The last item (Provider as Employer) is optional, depending on whether a provider employs assistants and/or substitutes.

Each item is comprised of 2 to 5 indicator strands, and each indicator strand is comprised of four indicators on a rubric of increasing quality. After each indicator is rated, strand by strand, the item is scored on a 7-point scale from inadequate to excellent.

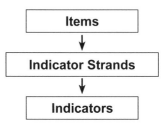

The following is a description of the ten items:

- **Qualifications and Professional Development** assesses the educational qualifications, ongoing professional development, and peer support of the provider.

- **Income and Benefits** looks at whether the provider increases tuition or fees to reflect changes in the cost of living, contracts with families for days of paid time off, and assesses access to health, retirement, or disability income benefits.

- **Work Environment** considers how well the space of the family child care home meets the needs of the enrolled children, the provider, and the provider's family. This item also assesses the adequacy of office and storage space used for the family child care business.

- **Fiscal Management** examines the availability of a current operating budget, policies and practices that ensure an adequate cash flow, evidence that standard accounting practices are adhered to, and that business income and expenses are reported to the IRS.

- **Recordkeeping** looks at whether the provider keeps track of income received, the number of meals and snacks served to children, caregiving and other business hours worked in the home, and additional business-related expenses.

- **Risk Management** assesses whether the family child care program has written policies and procedures that reduce risk, information displayed about emergency drills and emergency contact information, and whether the program has business liability insurance.

- **Provider-Family Communication** considers the content of the written contract the provider establishes with families, the completeness of written program policies, and the content of intake forms. This item also looks at the enrollment process and the variety of ways the provider communicates with families.

- **Family Support and Engagement** looks at whether the provider shares information with families about community resources and supports, including developmental screening services and the availability of financial assistance for child care. This item also assesses whether the provider offers informal and formal opportunities to discuss childrearing issues and sets goals for children's learning and development.

- **Marketing and Community Relations** evaluates the type and frequency of different external communication tools, how responsive the provider is to calls from prospective clients, and the provider's involvement in local business, civic, and religious organizations.

- **Provider as Employer** assesses the orientation of new employees (assistants and/or substitutes), how frequently employees meet with the provider to plan activities and share observations, and whether the provider pays employees at least the minimum wage, withholds federal taxes, and pays Social Security and Medicare taxes.

Definition of Terms

The following definitions should be used in completing the BAS:

Family child care	Child care that is offered in a home environment (a building designed and constructed to serve as a residence)
Family child care program	Includes the environment, the caregiving practices of the provider and any assistants, and the business practices of the provider
Family	Includes parents, grandparents, or guardians
Provider	The person responsible for planning, implementing, and evaluating the family child care program
CDA	Child Development Associate—a credential administered through the Council for Professional Recognition
GED	General Educational Development—a certificate of high school equivalency
sh	Semester hours of college credit
ECE/CD	Early childhood education or child development
Assistant	A person who works under the supervision of the provider and is not left in charge of children unless he or she meets all the qualifications of a substitute
Substitute	A person who is left in charge of children when the provider is absent and meets all licensing or registration requirements

Using the Business Administration Scale

Data Collection Procedures

The *Business Administration Scale for Family Child Care* (BAS) was designed for use by providers as a self-assessment tool, as well as for trained assessors such as researchers, technical assistance specialists, and program evaluators. Included for each item are pertinent notes providing clarification of the indicators. For updated notes, see the McCormick Center website: McCormickCenter.nl.edu.

Trained researchers, technical assistance specialists, and program evaluators using the BAS as a formal assessment tool should schedule approximately one hour to interview the provider and an additional hour for a review of documents. In advance of the visit, it is recommended that the provider receive a copy of the *Business Administration Scale for Family Child Care* and assemble the available documents for review, as noted on pages 30–31.

Upon arriving for the interview, the assessor should first ask the provider for a brief tour of the family child care home, including the indoor and outdoor child care spaces, space used for meeting with families, and any additional space designated for conducting the family child care business, such as office and storage areas.

Observations of the space used for the family child care program are needed to complete the rating of three items (Item 3, Work Environment; Item 6, Risk Management; and Item 9, Marketing and Community Relations). For the indicators needing documentation, the assessor should record a preliminary rating based on the statements made by the provider. After the interview, a thorough review of the content of the documents should be conducted and adjustments made to the rating of the indicators if necessary.

Scoring the BAS

Adhering to the following two rating principles for the *Business Administration Scale for Family Child Care* will promote consistency in scoring and accuracy in the BAS profile.

- In order to provide an accurate snapshot of business practices, it is important that ratings be based only on the indicators provided for each item. For some indicators, ratings are based solely on the provider's self-report (e.g., Item 1, Qualifications and Professional Development, Indicator 3.1). However, for most indicators it is necessary to review documents or make observations in order to verify the accuracy of the information. For these verifiable indicators, a "D" (document) or an "O" (observation) appears under the indicator number (e.g., Item 2, Income and Benefits, Indicator 5.3).

- Ratings should be based on existing policies and procedures, not past practices or plans for the future.

The following protocol should be used to score the *Business Administration Scale for Family Child Care:*

Step 1. Complete the Provider Qualifications Worksheet.

Only one person is designated as the Provider.

- The provider completes the Provider Qualifications Worksheet on page 32.

- Use this information to rate the indicators for Item 1, Qualifications and Professional Development.

Step 2. Rate the indicators for Items 1–10.

Use the following rules for rating the indicators:

- For each item, begin with the indicators under the 1 (inadequate) category and proceed across the continuum of quality in each indicator strand to 7 (excellent), writing in the spaces provided a Y (yes) or N (no).

- Record any supporting evidence in the margins near each indicator (e.g., an observation made of needed criteria).

Step 3. Determine scores for Items 1–10.

Use the following scoring rules for determining the item scores:

- A score of 1 is given if any indicator under the 1 column is rated Y (yes). A score of 1 is also given if all indicators under the 1 column are rated N (no) and less than half of the indicators under the 3 column are rated Y (yes).

- A score of 2 is given when all indicators under 1 are rated N (no) and at least half of the indicators under 3 are rated Y (yes).

- A score of 3 is given when all indicators under 1 are rated N (no) and all indicators under 3 are rated Y (yes).

- A score of 4 is given when all indicators under 1 are rated N (no), all indicators under 3 are rated Y (yes), and at least half of the indicators under 5 are rated Y (yes).

- A score of 5 is given when all indicators under 1 are rated N (no) and all indicators under 3 and 5 are rated Y (yes).

- A score of 6 is given when all indicators under 1 are rated N (no), all the indicators under 3 and 5 are rated Y (yes), and at least half of the indicators under 7 are rated Y (yes).

- A score of 7 is given when all indicators under 1 are rated N (no) and all indicators under 3, 5, and 7 are rated Y (yes).

Circle the item score in the space provided in the lower right-hand corner on each item page.

Step 4. Generate a Total BAS Score.

The Total BAS Score is the sum of the item scores. To calculate this score, transfer the individual item scores to the **Item Summary Form** (page 33). Sum the item scores for the entire scale.

- If the provider employs one or more assistants or substitutes, then 10 items are rated and the possible range of scores is 10–70.

- If the provider has no employees, then 9 items are rated and the possible range of scores is 9–63.

Step 5. Determine the Average BAS Item Score.

Use the **Item Summary Form** (page 33) to calculate the Average BAS Item Score which is the Total BAS Score divided by the number of items scored (a minimum of 9 for all family child care programs; 10 for family child care programs with one or more employees).

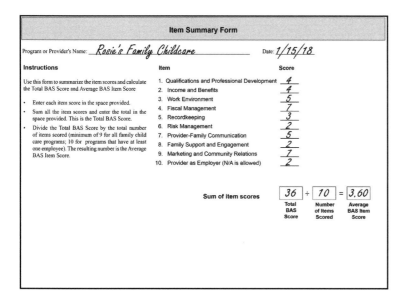

Step 6. Plot scores on the BAS Profile.

Plot the individual item scores on the graph of the **BAS Profile** (page 34); then connect the dots. Add the information at the bottom of the profile regarding the Total BAS Score, Number of Items Scored, and Average BAS Item Score.

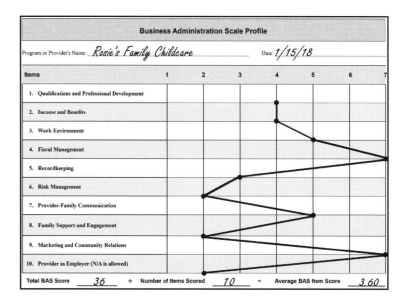

Business Administration Scale

Items

1. Qualifications and Professional Development

2. Income and Benefits

3. Work Environment

4. Fiscal Management

5. Recordkeeping

6. Risk Management

7. Provider-Family Communication

8. Family Support and Engagement

9. Marketing and Community Relations

10. Provider as Employer

1. Qualifications and Professional Development

Notes

Use the Provider Qualifications Worksheet on page 32 to record information regarding the provider's highest education level, specialized coursework and training, credentials, and family child care experience. This data can then be used to rate the indicators on the following page and generate a score for Item 1.

*   Business or management training **may** include:

❏ small business practices

❏ contracts

❏ recordkeeping

❏ tax planning

❏ legal and insurance issues

❏ business technology applications

❏ accounting

❏ marketing

❏ money management

❏ grant writing

❏ managing employees

❏ leadership and advocacy

❏ other _____

**   A network is three or more people that meet together (in-person or online) to provide mutual support of their work as family child care providers. The primary purpose of the meeting is peer support, not training.

***   A network of providers is considered formal if there are scheduled meetings and a record of proceedings is maintained.

****   An active role means that the provider regularly attends meetings or serves on a committee or workgroup. A leadership role means the provider chairs an event or committee, serves on an advisory/ governing board, or serves as an officer.

1. Qualifications and Professional Development

	1	2	3	4	5	6	7
	Inadequate		**Minimal**		**Good**		**Excellent**

___ 1.1 The provider does not have a high school diploma or GED.

___ 3.1 The provider has a minimum of a high school diploma or GED.

___ 5.1 The provider has a minimum of an associate degree or 60 sh of college credit.
D

___ 7.1 The provider has a minimum of a baccalaureate degree.
D

___ 1.2 The provider does not have a current CDA, Montessori credential (Early Childhood or Infant and Toddler), **or** a minimum of 6 sh of ECE/CD coursework.

___ 3.2 The provider has a current CDA, Montessori credential (Early Childhood or Infant and Toddler), **or** a minimum of 6 sh of college credit in ECE/CD.
D

___ 5.2 The provider has a minimum of 15 sh of ECE/CD coursework.
D

___ 7.2 The provider has a minimum of 24 sh of ECE/CD coursework.
D

___ 1.3 The provider has not attended any business or management training.*

___ 3.3 The provider has attended a minimum of 5 clock hours of business or management training.*
D

___ 5.3 The provider has attended a minimum of 10 clock hours of business or management training.*
D

___ 7.3 The provider has attended a minimum of 15 clock hours of business or management training.*
D

___ 1.4 The provider attended less than 15 clock hours of professional development during the last calendar year.

___ 3.4 The provider attended 15 or more clock hours of professional development during the last calendar year.
D

___ 5.4 The provider attended 30 or more clock hours of professional development during the last calendar year.
D

___ 7.4 The provider attended 45 or more clock hours of professional development during the last calendar year.
D

___ 1.5 The provider has no peer support.

___ 3.5 The provider has peer support through a network of providers.**

___ 5.5 The provider is a member of a formal network of providers or a family child care association.***
D

___ 7.5 The provider plays an active or leadership role in a formal network of providers or a family child care association.****
D

Rationale:

Circle the final score based on the scoring rules on pages 4–5.

1	2	3	4	5	6	7

1. Qualifications and Professional Development

2. Income and Benefits

Notes

*   Fees **may** include:

- ❒ tuition
- ❒ late fee
- ❒ registration fee
- ❒ extended-care fee
- ❒ fee for special services
- ❒ other _____

N/A is allowed **only** if the provisions for contracted care specifically prohibit the provider from charging families **any** fees **and** all the children in the provider's care are subject to such a contract. Contracted care refers to when a provider is paid by an agency rather than the family to provide child care.

**   Days of paid time off (e.g., vacation, sick leave, professional development, or personal days) are in addition to **six** commonly observed holidays which are paid in full by families (or sponsoring agency) when the contracted hours fall on these days. **Six** paid holidays are required to receive credit for any additional days of paid time off.

Paid holidays **may** include:

- ❒ New Year's Day
- ❒ Martin Luther King Jr. Day
- ❒ Presidents' Day
- ❒ Memorial Day
- ❒ Independence Day
- ❒ Labor Day
- ❒ Thanksgiving Day
- ❒ Christmas Day
- ❒ Other _____

***   A qualified retirement plan is a savings and investment plan that meets IRS requirements for favorable tax treatment (e.g., pretax contributions, tax deferred gains). A provider receiving social security retirement benefits (SSDI) still needs to contribute to a qualified retirement plan to receive credit for this indicator.

2. Income and Benefits

	1	2		3	4		5	6		7	
	Inadequate			**Minimal**			**Good**			**Excellent**	

___ 1.1 The provider has not increased or added a new fee charged to families within the last three years (N/A is allowed).*

___ 1.2 The provider does not receive at least 6 paid holidays per year.**

___ 1.3 The provider does not have health insurance.

___ 3.1 D The provider has increased or added a new fee charged to families within the last three years (N/A is allowed).*

___ 3.2 D The provider contracts with families (or sponsoring agency for contracted care) to receive a minimum of 3 **additional** days of paid time off per year.**

___ 3.3 D The provider has health insurance for self and dependent children.

___ 5.1 D The provider has increased or added a new fee charged to families within the last two years (N/A is allowed).*

___ 5.2 D The provider contracts with families (or sponsoring agency for contracted care) to receive a minimum of 5 **additional** days of paid time off per year.**

___ 5.3 D The provider has contributed to a qualified retirement plan during the past year.***

___ 7.1 D The provider has increased or added a new fee charged to families in each of the last three years (N/A is allowed).*

___ 7.2 D The provider contracts with families (or sponsoring agency for contracted care) to receive a minimum of 10 **additional** days of paid time off per year.**

___ 7.3 D The provider has disability income insurance.

Rationale:

Circle the final score based on the scoring rules on pages 4–5.

1   2   3   4   5   6   7

2. Income and Benefits

3. Work Environment

In a family child care program, the child care space may be restricted to a designated area of the home (e.g., basement, attached garage, or home addition) or it may include all or a majority of the space of the home.

*   Dual use of space may be considered adequate to meet the needs of both the enrolled children and the provider's family if the toys, equipment, and materials can be covered and/or contained at the end of the caregiving part of the day.

**   Defined office space **must** include:

    ☐ an adult-sized desk or work station

    ☐ an adult-sized chair

    ☐ file storage

***   The child care space **must** include one or more pieces of adult sized furniture primarily designed for comfort. A folding chair or desk chair does **not** meet this criteria.

****   The provider's posture and gestures demonstrate ease of access to all stored child care materials. The provider is able to fully grasp and remove stored objects without standing on tip-toes or using a chair, stool, or ladder.

3. Work Environment

1	2	3	4	5	6	7
Inadequate		**Minimal**		**Good**		**Excellent**

___ 1.1 The space is inadequate to meet the needs of both the enrolled children and the provider's family.*

___ 3.1
O   There is adequate space to meet the needs of both the enrolled children and the provider's family.*

___ 5.1
O   There is defined office space to conduct the family child care business.**

___ 7.1
O   The defined office space is equipped with a working computer, printer, copier, and Internet access.**

___ 1.2 There is no adult-sized chair, rocker, or sofa in the child care space of the home.***

___ 3.2
O   An adult-sized chair, rocker, or sofa is available in the child care space of the home.***

___ 5.2
O   There is natural light from a window or skylight in the child care space of the home.

___ 7.2
O   The storage space used for the program in the child care area of the home is at a height that promotes the health and safety of the provider.****

Rationale:

Circle the final score based on the scoring rules on pages 4–5.

    1   2   3   4   5   6   7

3. Work Environment

4. Fiscal Management

Notes

* An operating budget is a projection or plan for the amount of money that will be made (revenue) by the child care business and the amount of money that will be spent (expenditures) to operate the child care business during the fiscal year.

** Practices that provide for adequate cash flow **may** include:

❏ provision for families to make direct deposits or electronic payments

❏ clear policy and/or procedure regarding the collection of delinquent tuition/fees

❏ clear policy and/or procedure regarding termination of contract due to nonpayment of tuition/fees

❏ business form or invoice used to report tuition/fees owed

❏ quarterly cash-flow projections (anticipated revenue and expenditures summarized at three-month intervals and developed from the operating budget)

❏ other_____

*** A qualified tax preparer refers to a certified public accountant (CPA), an enrolled agent (EA), or other tax preparer with expertise in family child care taxes.

**** Types of expenses **may** include:

❏ food

❏ toys

❏ supplies

❏ rent

❏ mortgage interest

❏ utilities

❏ depreciation

❏ car

❏ property tax

❏ other_____

If a provider's business is incorporated, he or she would fill out either Form 1120 or 1120S. If the provider is incorporated as a single person LLC, then the tax forms to be filled out are the same as for a sole proprietor (Form 1040 Schedule C; Form 8829). If a provider is set up as a partnership, then the tax form to file is Form 1065.

4. Fiscal Management

1	2	3	4	5	6	7
Inadequate		**Minimal**		**Good**		**Excellent**

___ 1.1 An operating budget for the current year is not available.*

___ 3.1 D An operating budget for the current year is available.*

___ 5.1 D The operating budget for the current year has line-item breakdowns for revenue and expenditures.*

___ 7.1 D The operating budget for the current year projects a profit.*

___ 1.2 There is no policy requiring payment of tuition and/or fees in advance of care.

___ 3.2 D There is a written policy requiring payment of tuition and/or fees in advance of care (e.g., payment due on Monday for the current week).

___ 5.2 D There are two or more practices that provide for adequate cash flow.**

___ 7.2 D There are three or more practices that provide for adequate cash flow.**

___ 1.3 There is no review of accounting records.

___ 3.3 D There is a monthly review of accounting records (e.g., reconciliation of the bank statement; income compared to expenses).

___ 5.3 D The provider consults with a qualified tax preparer to assure compliance with reporting requirements and payment of taxes.***

___ 7.3 D Income and expenses are summarized on a quarterly basis and compared to quarterly cash-flow projections.

___ 1.4 The provider does not report income to the IRS.

___ 3.4 D The provider reports income to the IRS.

___ 5.4 D The provider claims at least three types of expenses on IRS Form 1040 Schedule C.****

___ 7.4 D The provider claims five or more types of expenses on IRS Form 1040 Schedule C.****

Rationale:

Circle the final score based on the scoring rules on pages 4–5.

1   2   3   4   5   6   7

4. Fiscal Management

5. Recordkeeping

Notes

* The end-of-year statement **must** include:

- ❏ provider's federal tax ID or social security number

- ❏ children's names for whom child care was provided and the total amount of money received for providing child care

- ❏ months in which care was provided during the calendar year

- ❏ signatures of the family/guardian and the provider

** The Child and Adult Care Food Program (CACFP), a program of the U.S. Department of Agriculture, reimburses child care providers for serving nutritious food to children under the age of 13 years. Meals served to children over 13, or not considered "credible" by CACFP (e.g., birthday cake), should still be recorded and counted as a tax deduction.

*** Expenses are 100% business-related if they are for supplies or services that are used exclusively in the family child care business. Some examples of exclusive expenses **may** include:

- ❏ supplies

- ❏ toys

- ❏ equipment

- ❏ advertising

- ❏ professional services

- ❏ association dues

- ❏ other_____

Expenses are shared if they are for supplies or services that are used in the family child care business and are also personally used by the provider or the provider's family. Some examples of shared expenses **may** include:

- ❏ food

- ❏ toilet paper

- ❏ cleaning and laundry supplies

- ❏ furniture

- ❏ toys

- ❏ mortgage interest/rent

- ❏ utilities

- ❏ home insurance

- ❏ real estate taxes

- ❏ home repair

- ❏ outdoor maintenance

- ❏ other_____

**** The Time-Space Percentage refers to the calculation used to determine the tax deduction allowed for the business use of the provider's home. The Time-Space Percentage is entered on IRS Form 8829 Expenses for Business Use of Your Home. (N/A is allowed only if the business has a legal status other than sole proprietorship or single person LLC).

5. Recordkeeping

	1		2		3		4		5		6		7
	Inadequate				**Minimal**				**Good**				**Excellent**

___ 1.1 The provider does not keep track of tuition, fees, and other income received.

___ 3.1 The provider keeps track of tuition, D fees, and other income received.

___ 5.1 The provider gives families an D end-of-the-year statement of tuition and/or fees paid.*

___ 7.1 The provider gives families a D receipt for each payment of tuition and/or fees.

___ 1.2 The provider does not keep track of the number of meals and snacks served to children.

___ 3.2 The provider keeps track of the D number of meals and snacks served to children.

___ 5.2 The provider participates in D the Food Program and submits monthly reports of the number of meals and snacks served to children that are reimbursed.**

___ 7.2 The provider keeps track D of the number of meals and snacks that are not reimbursed but are served to children.**

___ 1.3 The provider does not keep track of caregiving hours in the home.

___ 3.3 The provider keeps track of D caregiving hours in the home.

___ 5.3 The provider keeps track D of irregular or unscheduled caregiving hours in the home (e.g., child stays overnight, dropped off early, or picked up late).

___ 7.3 The provider keeps track D of business conducted and hours worked in the home when children are not present (e.g., paying bills, cleaning, curriculum planning).

___ 1.4 The provider does not keep track of business expenses.

___ 3.4 The provider keeps track of D expenses that are 100% business-related.***

___ 5.4 The provider keeps track of shared D expenses associated with the business use of the home.***

___ 7.4 The provider has reported the D Time-Space Percentage for shared expenses associated with the business use of the home (N/A is allowed).****

Rationale:

Circle the final score based on the scoring rules on pages 4–5.

1   2   3   4   5   6   7

5. Recordkeeping

6. Risk Management

Notes

*   Written policies that reduce risk from emergency situations **may** include written procedures to follow in the event of:

☐ fire

☐ severe storm or natural disaster

☐ power outage

☐ accident

☐ intruder

☐ other_____

Written policies that reduce the risk of child abuse and neglect allegations **may** include written procedures to:

☐ implement open-door policy

☐ notify family regarding minor accidents involving child

☐ implement daily health checks

☐ maintain daily sign-in and sign-out sheets

☐ other_____

Written policies to maintain the safety of people, property, equipment, and materials **may** include written procedures to ensure:

☐ universal precautions are followed

☐ annual replacement of smoke alarm batteries

☐ annual servicing of fire extinguisher

☐ routine sterilization of toys

☐ signed permission forms from families authorizing each field trip away from the home

☐ children are not released to anyone who appears to be under the influence of alcohol or drugs

☐ children are not released to anyone transporting children without an appropriate car seat or seatbelt

☐ other_____

**   A written risk management plan is a binder or notebook containing the written policies and procedures that reduce risk. The risk management plan can be a part of an operational binder or family handbook, but **must** be clearly labeled "risk management plan."

***   Emergency information **must** include the daytime numbers for families and any allergy and/or medical conditions of the children (credit is not received if information is stored only on an electronic device).

****   Business liability insurance provides coverage for accidents and lawsuits against the family child care business. Comprehensive business liability insurance **must** provide coverage for:

☐ professional liability (e.g., failure to meet standard of care; failure to supervise)

☐ legal defense in case of a lawsuit

☐ child abuse (both physical and sexual)

☐ medical costs of an injured child or parent

☐ personal injury

☐ accidents occurring away from the home (e.g., fieldtrips, walks)

6. Risk Management

1	2	3	4	5	6	7
Inadequate		**Minimal**		**Good**		**Excellent**

___ 1.1 There are no written policies that reduce risk.*

___ 3.1 D There are a minimum of three written policies that reduce risk.*

___ 5.1 D There are a minimum of five written policies that reduce risk.*

___ 7.1 D There is a written risk management plan that is reviewed annually.**

___ 1.2 The enrollment form does not ask for names and contact information for individuals authorized to pick up children.

___ 3.2 D The enrollment form asks for names and contact information for individuals authorized to pick up children.

___ 5.2 D Identification is verified for any unfamiliar person picking up children.

___ 7.2 D Children may leave the program with a person not authorized on the enrollment form only with written and signed notice in advance.

___ 1.3 During the past year, fire drills were not practiced at least once a month.

___ 3.3 D During the past year, fire and disaster drills were practiced at least once a month.

___ 5.3 O Fire and disaster drill records for the past twelve months are displayed or posted for families to see.

___ 7.3 D Displayed or posted fire and disaster drill records include the length of the drills and notes about improvements needed.

___ 1.4 There is no working phone (a land line or cell phone).

___ 3.4 O There is a working phone and emergency numbers are posted, including 911, poison control, and daytime phone numbers of families (can be posted in a confidential manner).

___ 5.4 O Emergency information is portable and taken with the provider any time children take walks, go on fieldtrips, or are transported.***

___ 7.4 O Information is posted regarding children's allergies and two backup contacts for families (can be posted in a confidential manner).

___ 1.5 The provider does not have business liability insurance.****

___ 3.5 D The provider has business liability insurance.****

___ 5.5 D The provider has comprehensive business liability insurance.****

___ 7.5 D The provider has business property insurance and, if the provider transports children, has commercial auto insurance.

Rationale:

Circle the final score based on the scoring rules on pages 4–5.

1   2   3   4   5   6   7

6. Risk Management

7. Provider-Family Communication

Notes

* Written program policies **may** include:

- ❐ discipline and guidance
- ❐ mandated reporting of child abuse and neglect
- ❐ daily routines
- ❐ items family must provide (e.g., diapers, formula, extra clothing)
- ❐ child illness
- ❐ drop off and pick up
- ❐ fieldtrips
- ❐ emergency closings
- ❐ developmental screening
- ❐ late pick up
- ❐ celebrations
- ❐ accident reports
- ❐ annual family evaluation
- ❐ other_____

** Documentation may be an enrollment form provided by the state plus a supplemental form developed by the provider. Background information **must** include:

- ❐ child's developmental history
- ❐ allergies and chronic medical conditions
- ❐ child's strengths, likes, and dislikes
- ❐ family preferences regarding childrearing practices (e.g., eating, sleeping, discipline, toileting).

*** A good fit is determined by a face-to-face exchange of information in which the provider explains the terms of the enrollment contract and program policies. Provider shares sample menus and contact information for two or more references.

**** Methods of communication **may** include:

- ❐ face-to-face conversation
- ❐ newsletter
- ❐ bulletin board
- ❐ note that goes home with children
- ❐ website
- ❐ e-mail
- ❐ phone call
- ❐ text message
- ❐ social media
- ❐ other_____

7. Provider-Family Communication

1	2	3	4	5	6	7
Inadequate		**Minimal**		**Good**		**Excellent**

___ 1.1 There is no written contract between the provider and the family (or between the provider and the sponsoring agency) paying for the child care services.

___ 3.1 D There is a written contract between the provider and the family (or between the provider and the sponsoring agency) paying for the child care services.

___ 5.1 D The written contract includes the names of the provider and family (or sponsoring agency) in the body of the contract, hours of care, payment terms, all additional fees, termination procedures, and signatures of both parties.

___ 7.1 D The written contract also includes information about rates during the provider's absences (e.g., sick/personal, holiday, and vacation days), the family's vacation, and the child's absences.

___ 1.2 There are no written program policies provided to families.*

___ 3.2 D There are at least five written program policies provided to families.*

___ 5.2 D There are at least seven written program policies provided to families.*

___ 7.2 D A family handbook containing at least nine program policies is provided to families and also includes the program philosophy, goals, and curriculum.*

___ 1.3 There is no intake form used to document background information about the child and family.

___ 3.3 D After a child is enrolled, an intake form is used to document background information about the child and family.**

___ 5.3 D Before making the enrollment decision, an effort is made to determine whether the provider and the family are a good fit.***

___ 7.3 D The enrollment process includes more than one visit by the family and child, providing a gradual transition.

___ 1.4 The provider does not speak the family's primary language or utilize resources to communicate.

___ 3.4 D The provider speaks the family's primary language or utilizes resources to communicate.

___ 5.4 D The provider communicates with families using five or more methods of communication.****

___ 7.4 D The provider communicates with families using seven or more methods of communication.****

Rationale:

Circle the final score based on the scoring rules on pages 4–5.

1   2   3   4   5   6   7

7. Provider-Family Communication

8. Family Support and Engagement

Notes

* Examples of community resources **may** include:

☐ child care resource and referral agency

☐ city recreation department

☐ public library

☐ housing authority

☐ family resource center

☐ crisis hotline

☐ Easter Seals

☐ public health clinic

☐ YMCA/YWCA

☐ recycling center

☐ consumer credit counseling

☐ Social Security Administration

☐ Child Find or developmental screening services available through local early intervention organizations and public schools

☐ other_____

** Supports **may** include:

☐ tax credit

☐ state child care subsidy (CCAP)

☐ private child care subsidy (sliding fee scale; second child discounted tuition)

☐ employer-sponsored child care benefit

☐ other_____

*** Child development and childrearing topics **may** include:

☐ language/literacy

☐ brain development

☐ school readiness

☐ guidance and discipline

☐ fussy eaters

☐ challenging behavior

☐ sibling rivalry

☐ other_____

**** Events hosted by the provider **may** include:

☐ family meeting (discussion of topic)

☐ holiday celebration

☐ family work day

☐ potluck/picnic

☐ fieldtrip

☐ other_____

1	2	3	4	5	6	7
Inadequate		**Minimal**		**Good**		**Excellent**

___ 1.1 The provider has no descriptive information regarding community resources to share with families.*

___ 3.1 D The provider has descriptive information regarding a minimum of two community resources to share with families.*

___ 5.1 D The provider has descriptive information regarding a minimum of four community resources to share with families, including developmental screening services for children.*

___ 7.1 D The provider has descriptive information to share with families regarding supports to help reduce child care costs.**

___ 1.2 The provider does not share written information with families on child development or childrearing topics.***

___ 3.2 D The provider shares written information with families on child development or childrearing topics.***

___ 5.2 D The provider meets individually (in-person, video chat, or phone) with families at least once a year to discuss their children's progress and mutually set goals.

___ 7.2 D The provider meets individually (in-person, video chat, or phone) with families at least twice a year to discuss their children's progress and mutually set goals.

___ 1.3 The provider does not facilitate any events for families to build community.****

___ 3.3 D The provider facilitates at least two events a year for families to build community.****

___ 5.3 D Families participate in a routine program activity (e.g., reading a book, helping with a cooking project).

___ 7.3 D Families participate in an at-home learning activity that the provider makes available (e.g., lending library of books, activities, games, or puzzles for families and children to do together).

Rationale:

Circle the final score based on the scoring rules on pages 4–5.

1   2   3   4   5   6   7

8. Family Support and Engagement

9. Marketing and Community Relations

Notes

*   Public relations tools **may** include:

❑ flyers

❑ brochures

❑ business cards

❑ logo

❑ letterhead stationery

❑ newsletter

❑ website

❑ banner

❑ promotional items (e.g., t-shirts, mugs, magnets, pens)

❑ signage

❑ social media site

❑ other _____

**   Safe and inviting means that the outside of the home appears to be in good repair (e.g., there is no peeling paint, broken window, or torn screen) and the inside of the home appears to be clean, uncluttered, and free of unpleasant odors.

***   The provider engages with organizations in the community that are **not** focused on early care and education or family child care. Examples of civic, business, or faith-based organizations in the community **may** include:

❑ Rotary International

❑ United Way

❑ Chamber of Commerce

❑ League of Women Voters

❑ YWCA/YMCA

❑ church, synagogue, mosque, temple

❑ PTA/PTO

❑ elementary, middle, or high school

❑ city or village hall

❑ public library

❑ recreation department

❑ other _____

****   An **active** role means that the provider regularly attends meetings or serves on a committee or workgroup. A **leadership** role means the provider chairs an event or committee, serves on an advisory/ governing board, or serves as an officer.

9. Marketing and Community Relations

1	2	3	4	5	6	7
Inadequate		**Minimal**		**Good**		**Excellent**

___ 1.1 The provider utilizes no public relations tools.*

___ 1.2 The provider does not have voicemail or an answering machine to record calls during child care hours.

___ 1.3 The provider's home does not appear safe and inviting.**

___ 1.4 The provider does not attend at least two events per year sponsored by one or more organizations in the community.***

___ 3.1 D The provider utilizes at least two public relations tools.*

___ 3.2 O The provider has voice mail or an answering machine to record calls during child care hours.

___ 3.3 O The provider's home appears safe and inviting.**

___ 3.4 The provider attends two or more events per year sponsored by one or more organizations in the community.***

___ 5.1 D The provider utilizes at least four public relations tools.*

___ 5.2 D The provider keeps a record of calls and responds to inquiries from prospective clients within one business day.

___ 5.3 O The provider's credentials and/or evidence of attendance at training are displayed (e.g., bulletin board, portfolio).

___ 5.4 D The provider plays an active role in at least one organization in the community.****

___ 7.1 D The provider utilizes six or more public relations tools.*

___ 7.2 D The provider keeps a record of all prospective clients who inquire and what follow-up action is taken.

___ 7.3 O The provider uses a visual display (scrapbook, bulletin board, or photo album), demonstrating the benefits of the program.

___ 7.4 D The provider plays a leadership role in at least one organization in the community.****

Rationale:

Circle the final score based on the scoring rules on pages 4–5.

1   2   3   4   5   6   7

9. Marketing and Community Relations

10. Provider as Employer (N/A is allowed)

Notes

For the purpose of completing the BAS, a provider is considered an employer if he or she has pays an individual to perform child care services and directs that individual in the details of how the child care work is to be performed.

If the provider has employed an assistant and/or substitute at any time during the past 12 months, then Item 10 should be rated and scored even if the assistant and/or substitute has left the program.

An **assistant** works under the supervision of the provider and is not left in charge of children unless he or she meets all the qualifications of a substitute.

A **substitute** is a person who is left in charge of children when the provider is absent and meets all licensing or registration requirements.

*   When rating 1.2–7.2, only consider substitutes who work 20 or more hours per month. N/A is allowed when rating 1.2–7.2 if the provider employs no assistants but does employ one or more substitutes, all working less than 20 hours per month.

**   There are special rules that may apply when the employee is the provider's child. For example, if the employed child is less than 18 years old, his or her wages are not subject to Social Security or Medicare taxes. However, the provider must still file Form 941 or Form 944 to report wages and issue Form W-2 and Form W-3 to report annual wages paid even if there are no payroll taxes owed.

10. Provider as Employer (N/A is allowed)

1	2	3	4	5	6	7
Inadequate		**Minimal**		**Good**		**Excellent**

___ 1.1 There is no orientation for assistants and/or substitutes.

___ 3.1 The orientation of assistants and/or substitutes includes a review of responsibilities and program policies and procedures.

___ 5.1 D The orientation of assistants and/or substitutes includes meeting children and families before assuming responsibilities.

___ 7.1 D The orientation of assistants and/or substitutes includes receipt of a written job description and written program policies and procedures.

___ 1.2 The provider does not meet with assistants and/or substitutes to share observations and plan activities together. (N/A is allowed).*

___ 3.2 D The provider meets at least quarterly with assistants and/or substitutes to share observations and plan activities together. (N/A is allowed).*

___ 5.2 D The provider meets at least monthly with assistants and/or substitutes to share observations and plan activities together. (N/A is allowed).*

___ 7.2 D The provider meets at least monthly when children are not present with assistants and/or substitutes to share observations and plan activities together. (N/A is allowed).*

___ 1.3 The provider does not pay assistants and/or substitutes at least the federal minimum wage (or state or local minimum wage if one exists).

___ 3.3 D The provider pays assistants and/or substitutes at least the federal minimum wage (or state or local minimum wage if one exists), withholds federal taxes, and pays the employer's share of Social Security and Medicare taxes.**

___ 5.3 D The provider pays for worker's compensation insurance covering assistants and/or substitutes.

___ 7.3 D There is a written employment agreement or salary scale for assistants and/or substitutes identifying a wage based on job responsibilities, education or training, and experience.

Rationale:

Circle the final score based on the scoring rules on pages 4–5.

1   2   3   4   5   6   7   N/A

10. Provider as Employer (N/A is allowed)

B A S

Business Administration Scale
Forms

Documents for Review

Provider Qualifications Worksheet

Item Summary Form

Business Administration Scale Profile

Documents for Review

To prepare for a BAS assessment, make available for review the following documents related to your family child care program. Check *yes* or *no* indicating whether you have the documents listed. **Please note, many providers do not have all the examples listed.**

Item	Document	Provider Yes	Provider No	Assessor Verified
1	Credentials and transcripts of college coursework	☐	☐	☐
	Certificates of attendance or professional development record indicating business or management training	☐	☐	☐
	Certificates of attendance or professional development record indicating training for the last calendar year	☐	☐	☐
	Evidence of membership; an active, or leadership role in a formal family child care network or association	☐	☐	☐
2	Evidence of tuition or fee or introduction of new fee increase within the last three years	☐	☐	☐
	Family contract (or contract with sponsoring agency)	☐	☐	☐
	Evidence of provider's benefits (health insurance for self and any dependent children, retirement plan, disability income insurance)	☐	☐	☐
4	Operating budget for current year	☐	☐	☐
	Evidence of practices that provide for adequate cash flow (e.g., payment required in advance of service, actions taken in response to delinquent payments, quarterly cash-flow projections)	☐	☐	☐
	Evidence of monthly reconciliation of bank statement; monthly income and expense statement	☐	☐	☐
	Quarterly income and expense statement	☐	☐	☐
	Evidence of consultation with qualified tax preparer regarding tax liability (within the last 12 months)	☐	☐	☐
	Income tax report claiming business expenses (e.g., IRS Form 1040 Schedule C; Form 1120, 1120S)	☐	☐	☐
5	Record of income received, receipts given to families for each payment of tuition/fees, and end-of-year statement of tuition/fees paid	☐	☐	☐
	Record of number of meals and snacks served; monthly reports to the Food Program (CACFP)	☐	☐	☐
	Record of caregiving hours and other business hours worked in the home when children not present	☐	☐	☐
	Record of business-related expenses and usage of the Time-Space Percentage (IRS Form 8829)	☐	☐	☐

Item	Document	Provider Yes	Provider No	Assessor Verified
6	Risk management plan or written policies/procedures that reduce the provider's risk of doing business (e.g., what to do in various emergency situations; how to reduce the risk of child abuse allegations; how to prevent the spread of disease; procedures for releasing children from care)	☐	☐	☐
	Child enrollment form	☐	☐	☐
	Record of emergency drills (past 12 months)	☐	☐	☐
	Business insurance policies (e.g., business liability, business property, and commercial auto insurance)	☐	☐	☐
7	Contract and handbook or written program policies for families	☐	☐	☐
	Intake form documenting background information on child and family	☐	☐	☐
	Written materials (e.g., sample menus, references) for families considering enrollment	☐	☐	☐
	Notes, texts, email, newsletters, and other ways to communicate with families	☐	☐	☐
8	Written materials about community resources for families, including developmental screening	☐	☐	☐
	Written information about tax credits, child care subsidies, and/or employer child care benefits	☐	☐	☐
	Written information for families about child development and childrearing topics	☐	☐	☐
	Record of family conferences, family meetings, and social events (past 12 months)	☐	☐	☐
	Evidence that families participate in routine program activity and/or in-home learning activity	☐	☐	☐
9	Public relations tools (e.g., stationery, flyers, brochure, newsletter, t-shirts)	☐	☐	☐
	Dated log/record of enrollment inquiries and follow-up actions taken	☐	☐	☐
	Evidence of involvement with organizations in the community that are not focused on early care and education or family child care	☐	☐	☐
10	Evidence of orientation of assistants and/or substitutes; evidence that orientation includes receipt of written job description and program policies and procedures	☐	☐	☐
	Written employment agreement (or salary scale) for assistants and/or substitutes identifying wage based on responsibilities, education or training, and experience	☐	☐	☐
	Record of meetings with assistants and/or substitutes to share child observations and plan activities	☐	☐	☐
	Evidence of payment of at least minimum wage, payroll taxes, and worker's compensation for assistants and/or substitutes	☐	☐	☐

Provider Qualifications Worksheet

Program name:_____ Provider's name:_____ Date:_____

Highest Education Level

High School/GED	☐	Major:_____
Some college coursework	☐	Major:_____
AA/AAS/AAT	☐	Major:_____
BA/BS	☐	Major:_____
MA/MS	☐	Major:_____
EdD/PhD	☐	Major:_____
	_____	Total semesters hours (sh) of college credit

Specialized ECE/CD Coursework

_____ Total sh of ECE/CD college credit

Specialized Business/Management Coursework and Training*

_____ Total sh of business/management college credit

_____ Total clock hours of business/management training

Credentials/Certification

❏ CDA ❏ Administrator Credential/FCC Credential

❏ Montessori Credential ❏ Early Childhood Educator Credential

❏ Other: _____

Family Child Care Experience

_____ years _____ months

*Examples of business or management coursework/training may include: small business practices, contracts, recordkeeping, tax planning, legal and insurance issues, business technology applications, accounting, marketing, money management, grant writing, managing employees, and leadership and advocacy.

Item Summary Form

Program or Provider's Name: _____   Date: _____

Instructions

Use this form to summarize the item scores and calculate the Total BAS Score and Average BAS Item Score

- Enter each item score in the space provided.
- Sum all the item scores and enter the total in the space provided. This is the Total BAS Score.
- Divide the Total BAS Score by the total number of items scored (minimum of 9 for all family child care programs; 10 for programs that have at least one employee). The resulting number is the Average BAS Item Score.

Item	Score
1. Qualifications and Professional Development	_____
2. Income and Benefits	_____
3. Work Environment	_____
4. Fiscal Management	_____
5. Recordkeeping	_____
6. Risk Management	_____
7. Provider-Family Communication	_____
8. Family Support and Engagement	_____
9. Marketing and Community Relations	_____
10. Provider as Employer (N/A is allowed)	_____

Sum of item scores

Total BAS Score ÷ Number of Items Scored = Average BAS Item Score

Business Administration Scale Profile

Program or Provider's Name: _____   Date: _____

Items	1	2	3	4	5	6	7
1. Qualifications and Professional Development							
2. Income and Benefits							
3. Work Environment							
4. Fiscal Management							
5. Recordkeeping							
6. Risk Management							
7. Provider-Family Communication							
8. Family Support and Engagement							
9. Marketing and Community Relations							
10. Provider as Employer (N/A is allowed)							

Total BAS Score _____ ÷ **Number of Items Scored** _____ = **Average BAS Item Score** _____

Business Administration Scale

Appendices

- **Psychometric Characteristics of the BAS**

- **References and Resources**

- **About the Authors**

Psychometric Characteristics of the BAS

Psychometric Criteria

The development of the *Business Administration Scale for Family Child Care* (BAS) was guided by six psychometric criteria:

1. The BAS should demonstrate good internal consistency among the items.

2. The BAS should measure distinct, but related, business practices in family child care programs.

3. The BAS should demonstrate good inter-rater reliability.

4. The BAS should be applicable for use in family child care programs of varying sizes and in different geographic regions of the United States.

5. The BAS should be able to differentiate low- and high-quality programs.

6. The BAS should be related to, but not redundant with, similar measures of family child care program quality.

Sample

An initial reliability and validity study of the BAS was conducted in early 2007 with 64 family child care providers in Illinois. Data generated from this initial sample were used to make revisions in the wording of different indicators, delete redundant items, and streamline the data-collection protocol.

The sample for the 2009 reliability and validity study of the BAS (Sample #1) was drawn from 83 family child care providers in Florida, Tennessee, California, and Illinois. These states were selected as they varied in the stringency of state licensing regulations that govern family child care and provided a diverse national sample of providers. Providers were located in urban, suburban, and rural geographic regions of their state.

In each of the states, a local quality improvement technical assistance agency was contacted to assist with the data collection. Individuals with expertise in early childhood education were trained to administer the BAS. Technical assistance agencies were asked to recruit family child care programs that ranged in size and in quality. The BAS requires that providers document many business practices considered personal in nature. Consequently, the sample drew from providers who had previously established relationships with their local technical assistance agencies. These providers were assumed to be more willing to provide documentation and to participate in quality improvement activities than providers who had no prior relationships with their local technical assistance agencies.

While Sample #1 does not reflect the overall population of providers in the United States, it does represent the providers who would be most likely to use the BAS for quality improvement purposes. Each provider was given a list of documents needed to fulfill each BAS criterion several weeks prior to the BAS administration by an independent observer. Table 1 presents information on the characteristics of programs comprising Sample #1.

The mean licensed capacity of the family child care programs included in Sample #1 was 11.6 children, with providers enrolling an average of 8.3 full-time children and 1.5 part-time children. Eighty-eight percent of the sample served at least 6 children, with over 43% of the sample considered large programs serving at least 11 children.

With the publication of the 2018 second edition of the BAS, updated national norms were generated. The data comprising Sample #2 represent 439 family child care programs in 22 states that had a certified BAS assessor conduct an assessment between 2009 and 2017.

As can be seen in Table 2, most providers enrolled infants, toddlers, and preschoolers, with nearly 52% enrolling school-aged children.

Table 1. *Sample #1 Characteristics*

Number of Children Served by Age ($N = 606$)*					
Birth–2.11 years		3–4.11 years		5–12 years	
N	%	N	%	N	%
204	33.7	256	42.2	146	24.1
Number of Programs Serving Age Groups ($N = 64$)*					
Birth–2.11 years		3–4.11 years		5–12 years	
N	%	N	%	N	%
62	96.9	60	93.8	39	60.9
Program Size					
Small (1–5 children)		Medium (6–10 children)		Large (11–16 children)	
N	%	N	%	N	%
10	12	37	44.6	36	43.4

Note. *19 programs did not provide information on age and number of children served

Table 2. *Sample #2 Characteristics*

Number of Children Served by Age ($N = 3,897$)					
Birth–2.11 years		3–4.11 years		5–12 years	
N	%	N	%	N	%
1,193	30.6	1,843	47.3	861	22.1
Number of Programs Serving Age Groups ($N = 439$)					
Birth–2.11 years		3–4.11 years		5–12 years	
N	%	N	%	N	%
339	77.2	354	80.6	227	51.7
Program Size					
Small (1–5 children)		Medium (6–10 children)		Large (11+ children)	
N	%	N	%	N	%
126	28.7	161	36.7	152	34.6

The mean licensed capacity of the family child care programs included in Sample #2 was 10.7 children. Seventy-one percent of the sample served at least 6 children, with over 34% of the sample considered large programs serving at least 11 children.

Reliability and Validity

Content validity. Initial content validity for the *Business Administration Scale for Family Child Care* was established by a panel of seven early childhood experts who evaluated each item and indicator to ensure that key business management practices of a family child care program were included. Content reviewers were asked to respond to the following questions and provide feedback:

- Do the items cover the most important areas of business management in family child care settings?

- Do the indicators under each item adequately represent each item?

- Do the indicators appropriately show increasing levels of quality on a continuum?

- Does the wording of the item headings adequately reflect their content?

Multiple refinements were made to the wording and layout of the 2009 edition of the BAS as a result of initial feedback provided by the reviewers. Additional revisions were made from feedback received by assessors who collected data in the initial reliability and validity study and through data analysis. As a result, the wording and order of some indicators was changed and redundant items removed to assure that the BAS was applicable to a full range of family child care programs. Refinements made for the second edition of the BAS represent ongoing feedback from assessors and practitioners to ensure that the tool is current and to reduce any ambiguity in the interpretation of criteria.

Descriptive statistics. The BAS was constructed as one overall scale that measures the quality of family child care business and professional practices. The scale is made up of 37 indicator strands organized into 10 items scored on a 7-point Likert scale. An overall BAS score is calculated by taking the average of all items scored in the entire scale. For providers who have employees, 10 items are used to derive the total BAS score. For providers without employees, only the first 9 items are included in the overall BAS score. Table 3 provides the mean scores and standard deviations for the 10 items rated on the BAS and for the total BAS score.

Table 3. *Mean Scores and Standard Deviations for BAS Items Sample #1 (N = 83), Sample #2 (N = 439)*

Item #	Item	Indicator Strands	Sample #1		Sample #2	
			M	SD	M	SD
1	Qualifications and Professional Development	5	3.60	1.73	3.26	2.03
2	Income and Benefits	3	2.93	1.96	2.78	1.95
3	Work Environment	2	5.87	1.67	5.94	1.83
4	Fiscal Management	4	2.31	2.15	2.50	2.28
5	Recordkeeping	4	3.83	2.09	4.09	1.95
6	Risk Management	5	2.84	1.62	3.03	1.85
7	Provider-Family Communication	4	4.83	2.08	3.69	2.08
8	Family Support and Engagement	3	3.99	2.05	3.60	1.94
9	Marketing and Community Relations	4	4.88	1.64	3.91	1.74
10	Provider as Employer [†]	3	2.48	1.57	2.60	1.69
	Total BAS	37	3.78	1.03	3.59	1.16

Note. [†] *N* for Sample 1 = 65. *N* for Sample 2 = 230.

Distribution of scores. Each BAS item score and the total BAS score is rated on a 1–7 Likert scale, with 1 indicating inadequate business practices, 3 indicating minimal quality practices, 5 indicating good quality practices, and 7 indicating excellent business practices. Table 4 reports the distribution of BAS item scores by quality level in Sample #1.

As can be seen in this table, Item 3, Work Environment has a distribution of scores concentrated at the high end of the scale. This may be due in part to the fact that this item has only two indicator strands, reducing the possibility for variability. Further review by experts determined that this item had face validity and was an important quality construct and should remain in the BAS. Conversely, Item 4, Fiscal Management has a distribution of scores concentrated at the lower end of the scale.

Total BAS scores ranged from 1.88 to 6.40. This, as well as the distribution of scores detailed in Table 3, suggests that the BAS has an acceptable distribution of item scores and overall BAS scores across the quality continuum.

Internal consistency. Since the items in the BAS are organized under one common factor, a Cronbach's Alpha was conducted to determine how well the set of items measure the unidimensional construct. Coefficient alpha for Sample #1 for the total 10-item scale ($n = 65$) was calculated at .77, and for the 9-item scale ($n = 83$) at .73, indicating that the BAS has acceptable

Table 4. *Distribution of BAS Item Scores by Quality Level (N = 83)*

Item #	Item Score			
	1	2–3	4–5	6–7
1	22%	11%	50%	17%
2	41%	13%	36%	10%
3	4%	2%	24%	70%
4	64%	13%	2%	21%
5	27%	7%	32%	34%
6	22%	42%	26%	10%
7	13%	10%	22%	55%
8	12%	32%	25%	31%
9	6%	5%	46%	43%
10	35%	40%	19%	6%
Mean	24.6%	17.5%	28.2%	29.7%

internal consistency among items and that the items reliably measure the construct. Coefficient alpha for Sample #2 for the total 10-item scale ($n = 230$) was calculated at .81, and for the 9-item scale ($n = 439$) at .78, again demonstrating acceptable internal consistency among items.

Distinctiveness of items. The 10 BAS items were correlated to determine the extent to which they measure distinct, though somewhat related, aspects of family child care business practices. Table 5 reports the results of the Pearson's r correlational analysis between items. Coefficients ranged from .01 to .44, confirming that individual items on the BAS measure distinct, yet somewhat related, characteristics of family child care business practices.

Inter-rater reliability. Inter-rater reliability, the degree to which assessors' item scores match the BAS anchors' scores, was determined during a four-day training on the use of the instrument with 21 assessors. Using videotaped interviews and a review of sample documentation for the entire data collection process, assessors were rated on how often they matched the BAS anchors' scores within 1 point on each item. Individual assessor inter-rater reliability scores ranged from 90% to 100% agreement on the 10 BAS items. Overall average inter-rater reliability for the 21 assessors was 94%. Individual item reliability scores ranged from 67% to 100%, with the median item reliability score calculated at 100% agreement.

Differentiating programs. To assure that the BAS is applicable for use in programs of varying sizes, an analysis of variance (ANOVA) was conducted. Programs were considered large in size if the provider served 11 or more children. Large programs constituted 43% of Sample #1.

The results in Table 6 provide confirmatory evidence that average scores on the BAS do not vary based on the size of a provider's program. Providers of larger programs scored similarly ($M = 4.00$, $SD = 1.09$) to those of smaller programs ($M = 3.61$, $SD = .97$). Additionally, for 9 of the 10 items, no significant differences in BAS scores based on program size were found. Item 10, Provider as Employer demonstrated slightly higher scores for larger programs

Table 5. *BAS Item Intercorrelations (N = 83)*

Item	1	2	3	4	5	6	7	8	9	10
1. Qualifications and Professional Development	--	.20	.07	.21	.14	.33	.01	.38	.25	.23
2. Income and Benefits			.11	.30	.39	.15	.44	.34	.28	.42
3. Work Environment				.23	.21	.13	.22	.01	.22	.03
4. Fiscal Management					.40	.11	.14	.19	.27	.29
5. Recordkeeping						.08	.27	.28	.39	.32
6. Risk Management							.20	.33	.20	.15
7. Provider-Family Communications								.30	.17	.22
8. Family Support and Engagement									.29	.36
9. Marketing and Community Relations										.44
10. Provider as Employer										--

($M = 2.85$, $SD = 1.88$) than for smaller programs ($M = 2.06$, $SD = 1.03$), with an F calculated at 4.28 with $p = .04$.

To assure that the BAS is applicable for use in different geographic regions, an analysis of variance was conducted to determine whether average BAS scores varied based on the state in which a provider operates. The results in Table 7 provide evidence that BAS scores do not significantly vary based on geographic region. Additionally, for 8 of the 10 items, no significant differences in BAS item scores were found. For Item 2, Income and Benefits, post hoc tests revealed that programs in California scored higher than those in Florida. For Item 7, Provider-Family Communication, post hoc tests found that programs in California and Tennessee scored higher than those in Florida and Illinois.

Table 6. *Analysis of Variance by Program Size (N = 83)*

	Sum of Squares	df	Mean Square	F	p <
Between groups	3.058	1	3.058	2.924	.091
Within groups	84.719	81	1.046		
Total	**87.776**	**82**			

Table 7. *Analysis of Variance by Geographic Region (N = 83)*

	Sum of Squares	df	Mean Square	F	p <
State	6.113	3	2.038	1.971	.125

In order to determine if the BAS adequately differentiates between programs of varying quality, the *Family Child Care Environment Rating Scale–Revised* (FCCERS-R) (Harms, Cryer, & Clifford, 2007) was administered to a subsample of 33 providers. The FCCERS-R is a 38-item measure of global family child care quality that rates programs on a 1–7 Likert scale with 1 considered inadequate and 7 considered excellent. For the current analysis, programs were grouped into those that scored at or below 3.50 (the mid-point of the scale) and those that scored higher than 3.50. Eighteen programs scored above 3.50 while 15 scored at or below 3.50. An analysis of variance (ANOVA) was then conducted. The results presented in Table 8 provide evidence that lower-quality programs scored significantly lower on the BAS ($M = 3.08$, $SD = .89$) than programs with higher global quality ($M = 3.87$, $SD = .94$).

Concurrent validity. Concurrent validity for the BAS was determined by a correlational analysis with one subscale of the FCCERS-R that measures organizational effectiveness—the Parents and Provider subscale. Seventy-eight of the providers in the sample were administered the Parents and Provider subscale of the FCCERS-R. Table 9 demonstrates moderate correlations with this subscale of the FCCERS-R, confirming that the BAS measures related (but not redundant) characteristics of program quality as measured on the FCCERS-R.

Table 8. *Analysis of Variance by Overall Program Quality (N = 33)*

	Sum of Squares	df	Mean Square	F	p <
Between groups	5.175	1	5.175	6.103	.019
Within groups	26.285	31	.848		
Total	**31.460**	**32**			

The results of the reliability and validity study support the conclusion that the BAS has achieved all six psychometric criteria: it demonstrates good internal consistency; measures somewhat distinct but related business and professional practices of family child care; has good inter-rater reliability; does not unfairly discriminate against programs of varying sizes or located in different geographic regions; can differentiate between quality levels as measured by the FCCERS–R; and is related to, but not redundant with, other measures of program quality.

Table 9. *Correlation of BAS Items with FCCERS-R Parents and Provider Subscale (N = 78)*

BAS Item	FCCERS-R Parents and Provider Subscale
1. Qualifications and Professional Development	.29*
2. Income and Benefits	.32*
3. Work Environment	.15
4. Fiscal Management	.19
5. Recordkeeping	.16
6. Risk Management	.36*
7. Provider-Family Communication	.44**
8. Family Support and Engagement	.38**
9. Marketing and Community Relations	.20
10. Provider as Employer [†]	.21
Average BAS Score	**.49****

Note. [†] $N = 65$. $N = 6$. $*p < .05$. $**p < .01$.

References and Resources

Abell, E., Arsiwalla, D., Putnam, R., & Miller, E. (2014). Mentoring and facilitating professional engagement as quality enhancement strategies: An overview and evaluation of the Family Child Care Partnerships program. *Child Youth Care Forum, 43*, 569–592. doi: 10.1007/s10566-014-9254-1

Bordin, J., Machida, S., & Varnell, H. (2000, October). The relation of quality indicators to provider knowledge of child development in family child care homes. *Child and Youth Care Forum, 29*(5), 323–341.

Bromer, J., & Weaver, C. (2016). Supporting family child care and quality improvement: Findings from an exploratory survey of Illinois child care resource and referral agency staff. *International Journal of Child Care and Education Policy*. doi: 10.1186/s40723-016-0020-8

Copeland, T. (2014). *Family child care record-keeping guide* (9th ed.). St. Paul, MN: Redleaf Press.

Copeland, T. (2008). *Family child care business planning guide*. St. Paul, MN: Redleaf Press.

Copeland, T. (2008). *Family child care money management and retirement guide*. St. Paul, MN: Redleaf Press.

Copeland, T. (2006). *Family child care contracts and policies: How to be businesslike in a caring profession*. St. Paul, MN: Redleaf Press.

Copeland, T., & Millard, M. (2004). *Family child care legal and insurance guide: How to reduce the risks of running your business*. St. Paul, MN: Redleaf Press.

Dischler, P. (2005). *From babysitter to business owner: Getting the most out of your home child care business*. St. Paul, MN: Redleaf Press.

Fischer, J. L., & Eheart, B. K. (1991). Family day care: A theoretical basis for improving quality. *Early Childhood Research Quarterly, 6*(4), 549–563.

Forry, N., Iruka, I., Tout, K., Torquati, J., Susman-Stillman, A., Bryant, D., & Daneri, M. P. (2013). Predictors of quality and child outcomes in family child care settings. *Early Childhood Research Quarterly, 28*(4), 893–904.

Gerstenblatt, P., Faulkner, M., Lee, A., Doanm K. T., & Travis, D. (2014). Not babysitting: Work stress and well-being for family child care providers. *Early Childhood Education Journal, 42*, 67–75. doi: 10.1007/s10643-012-0571-4

Goleman, H., Shapiro, E., & Pence, A. R. (1990). Family environment and family day care. *Family Relations, 39*(1), 14–19.

Hallam, R., Bargreen, K., & Ridgley, R. (2013). Quality in family child care settings: The relationship between provider educational experiences and global quality scores in a statewide quality rating and improvement system. *Journal of Research in Childhood Education, 27*, 393–406.

Hamm, K., Gault, B., & Jones-DeWeever, A. (2005). *In our own backyards: Local and state strategies to improve the quality of family child care*. Washington, DC: Institute for Women's Policy Research.

Harms, T., Cryer, D., & Clifford, R. (2007). *Family Child Care Environment Rating Scale – Revised*. New York, NY: Teachers College Press.

Helburn, S. W., Morris, J. R., & Modigliani, K. (2002). Family child care finances and their effect on quality and incentives. *Early Childhood Research Quarterly, 17*(4), 512–538.

References and Resources

Hemmeter, M. L., Joseph, G. E., Smith, B. J., & Sandall, S. (Eds.). (2001). *DEC recommended practices program assessment: Improving practices for young children with special needs and their families.* Longmont, CO: Sopris West.

Hughes-Belding, K., Hegland, S., Stein, A., Sideris, J., & Bryant, D. (2012). Predictors of global quality in family child care homes: Structural and belief characteristics. *Early Education and Development, 23*(5), 697–712. doi: 10.1080/10409289.2011.574257

Jack, G. (2005). *The business of child care: Management and financial strategies.* Clifton Park, NY: Thomson Delmar Learning.

Kelton, R., Talan, T. N., & Bloom, P. J. (2013, Fall). Alternative pathways in family child care quality rating and improvement systems. *Early Childhood Research & Practice, 15*(2).

Kontos, S., Howes, C., & Galinsky, E. (1996). Does training make a difference to quality in family child care? *Early Childhood Research Quarterly, 11,* 427–445.

Kontos, S., Howes, C., Shinn, M., & Galinsky, E. (1995). *Quality in family child care and relative care.* New York, NY: Teachers College Press.

Lanigan, J. (2011). Family child care providers' perspectives regarding effective professional development and their role in the child care system: A qualitative study. *Early Childhood Education Journal, 38,* 399–409. doi: 10.1007/s10643-010-0420-2

Layzer, J. I., & Goodson, B. D. (2006). *National study of child care for low-income families: Care in the home: A description of family child care and the experiences of the families and children who use it.* Washington, DC: United States Department of Health and Human Services, Administration for Children and Families.

National Association for Family Child Care. (2013). *Quality standards for NAFCC accreditation* (4th ed.). Salt Lake City, UT: Author.

Ota, C., & Austin, A. (2013). Training and mentoring: Family child care providers use of linguistic inputs in conversations with children. *Early Childhood Research Quarterly, 28*(4), 972–983.

Raikes, H., Raikes, H., & Wilcox, B. (2005). Regulation, subsidy receipt and provider characteristics: What predicts quality in child care homes? *Early Childhood Research Quarterly, 20,* 164–184.

Raikes, H., Torquati, J., Jung, E., Peterson, C., Atwater, J., Scott, J., & Messner, L. (2013). Family child care in four Midwestern states: Multiple measures of quality and relations to outcomes by licensed status and subsidy program participation. *Early Childhood Research Quarter, 28*(4), 879–892.

Susman-Stillman, A., Pleuss, J., & Englund, M. (2013). Attitudes and beliefs of family- and center-based child care providers predict differences in caregiving behavior over time. *Early Childhood Research Quarterly, 28*(4), 905–917.

Talan, T. N., & Bloom, P. J. (2011). *Program Administration Scale: Measuring Early Childhood Leadership and Management* (2nd ed.). New York, NY: Teachers College Press.

Weaver, R. H. (2002). Predictors of quality and commitment in family child care: Provider education, personal resources, and support. *Early Education and Development, 13*(3), 265–282. doi: 10.1207/s15566935eed1303 2.

About the Authors

Teri N. Talan, Ed.D., J.D.

Teri N. Talan is Michael W. Louis Endowed Chair and Senior Policy Advisor at the McCormick Center for Early Childhood Leadership and professor of Early Childhood Education at National Louis University in Wheeling, Illinois. She represents the McCormick Center in public policy forums and promotes action by state and national policymakers on early childhood education and program administration issues. Previously, Dr. Talan was the executive director of an NAEYC-accredited early childhood program. She holds a law degree from Northwestern University and received a master's degree in Early Childhood Leadership and Advocacy and a doctoral degree in Adult Education from National Louis University. Dr. Talan's research interests are in the areas of early childhood workforce development, program quality evaluation, leadership, and systems integration. She is co-author of the *Program Administration Scale* (PAS), *Who's Caring for the Kids? The Status of the Early Childhood Workforce in Illinois,* and *Closing the Leadership Gap.*

Paula Jorde Bloom, Ph.D.

Paula Jorde Bloom was professor emerita at National Louis University and founder of the McCormick Center for Early Childhood Leadership at National Louis University in Wheeling, Illinois. She received her master's and doctoral degrees from Stanford University. Dr. Bloom's research interests were in the areas of organizational climate, occupational stress, job satisfaction, staff development, and other early childhood workforce issues. She authored numerous journal articles and several widely read books, including *Avoiding Burnout, A Great Place to Work, Blueprint for Action, Circle of Influence, Making the Most of Meetings, Workshop Essentials, Leadership in Action, Inspiring Peak Performance,* and *From the Inside Out.* She developed several assessment tools, including the *Early Childhood Work Environment Survey* (ECWES), the *Early Childhood Job Satisfaction Survey* (ECJSS), and with Teri Talan, the *Program Administration Scale (*PAS).